What Teens and Parents Need to Know

About Sex Offenders

with a Special Section about Internet Safety

Bobbie G. Hopes, Ph.D.

Avisson Press Inc.

Greensboro

First Edition
Printed in the USA

LCCN 2007928578

Trade Paperback
ISBN 10 : 1-888105-80-1
ISBN 13 : 978-1-888105-80-3

Library Binding
ISBN 10: 1-888105-79-8
ISBN 13: 978-1-888105-79-7

Contents

Introduction

Sex offenses against children, adolescents, and adults are this country's latest epidemic, and the damage caused by these offenses is far-reaching. At least 1 in 5 girls and 1 in 7 boys will be sexually abused before the age of 18, and most of the offenders are people whom the victim aready knows and trusts. However, increasing numbers of sex offenders are flocking to the Internet to troll for victims without ever leaving their homes or offices. These strangers are entering our homes via the Internet, and naive children and teens are their primary targets.

The increase of sex crimes in the U.S. has resulted in many new laws that were designed to help protect families and children from these predators. On May 17, 1996, President Clinton signed Megan's Law, which requires states to keep sexual offender registries and initiate community notification. However, each state has developed its own version of Megan's law, and the details vary from state to state.

Although there is some evidence that the rate of sex offenses has decreased since the enactment of these new laws, a broader solution to the problem is increased education and communication. Parents need to educate themselves about the signs that someone may be a sexual predator, parents and children need to talk with each other about it, and potential victims need to learn to protect themselves from these predators. This book begins that process by inspecting the mind of a sexual predator, by providing warning signs that someone may be a child molester, and by describing step-by-step instructions on how to avoid becoming the next victim of an Internet predator.

B.G.H.
March, 2007

The Basics

Sex offenses seem to be epidemic in today's culture, and the damage caused by these offenses has resulted in many new laws designed to help protect families and children from these predators. Approximately 1 in 5 girls and 1 in 7 boys will be sexually abused before they reach they reach 18. That's right, not 1 in 100, but 1 in 5 and 1 in 7. Some experts claim even higher rates of sexual abuse of children and adolescents.

Some Facts About Child Molesters

Most parents warn their children about the stranger who tries to lure them into a car, but what they don't realize is that the real danger is usually closer to home. In 90% of cases of child molestation, the child knows and trusts the person who commits the offense. Most victims are sexually molested by someone they know, most often a family member, close family friend or neighbor. The following list of the relationships between sex offenders and their victims and the percentage of sex offense cases that they comprise may surprise some people:

Acquaintances	36%
Other relatives	22%
Fathers, stepfathers	15%
Live-in boyfriends	10%
Strangers	10%
Brothers	7%

As you can see, in addition to fathers and stepfathers, mom's live-in boyfriends are also responsible for a large number of sex offenses within the ostensive family. Fathers and stepfathers comprise approximately 15% of sex offenses, while mom's live-in boyfriends comprise an additional 10%. The "brothers" category may surprise some. Please note that this is not referring to normal sex play between siblings.

Surprisingly, up to 20% of all rapes and 50% of all sex offenses are committed by juveniles, most of whom are between the ages of 13 and 17, although some are even younger.

What is a Pedophile?

Most parents mistakenly believe that pedophiles have no sexual interest in adults, and they never date or get married. In reality, only a small percentage of child molesters are attracted exclusively to children, but these are the most dangerous offenders, because they usually have many child victims over their lifetimes. Some pedophiles have reported having hundreds of victims. These offenders are called "fixated pedophiles." The term "fixated" refers to the fact that the offender's sexual interest in children is exclusive. The fixated pedophile is interested only in children. He is usually a single man who has never been married and never lived with a woman. He lives alone or may still live with his mother, regardless of his age.

If married, the marriage is a facade designed to hide his true intentions from potential victims and their families. In these rare cases when a fixated pedophile is married, his wife is usually physically or mentally impaired. This facade has the added benefits of gaining him a certain degree of compassion from people who see how tenderly he treats his poor wife. The fixated pedophile is the stereotype that most people have in mind, when they think of a child molester. They comprise only about 10% of all sex offenders, but they are the most dangerous.

The most common type of child molester is the "regressed pedophile." This type of offender typically has a history of voluntary, consensual sexual relationships with adult men or women, but during a period of significant stress in their lives, they "regress" in their sexual behavior and choose a child as their object of sexual attraction or desire. Common life stressors that result in this type of regressive behavior may include medical problems, loss of a job that was very important to him, marital problems, financial problems, or other serious problems that cause a significant setback in the way that the person views himself.

The most common type of regressed pedophile is the aging heterosexual male, who has had consensual adult sexual relationships throughout his life. Then, quite out of character for him, he begins to engage in sexual behavior toward a young child within the family. This behavior often follows retirement from his job or a serious medical problem, such as a heart attack or diabetes, which may also result in sexual dysfunction. He experiences a major loss of his previous role within the family, the loss of his previous sense of himself as a strong provider and protector, feelings of inferiority and anxiety about his health, and a deteriorating sense of importance to others in his life.

Most often, this is a father, stepfather, uncle, or grandfather, who chooses the child in the family whom he loves the most, then convinces himself that his actions are based in love. The offender may also be the trusted neighbor, teacher, or anyone else who has access to children.

Both sexual and emotional relationships with adult sexual partners are much more demanding and complicated than relationships with a child. Adults expect their partners to take an interest in their needs and to make an attempt to meet their partner's psychological and sexual needs in a responsible manner. When a man feels inadequate to meet these demands, turning to a child is safer and easier, because children are much more accepting and less demanding. The adult in crisis takes advantage of the child's gullibility and desire to please, and these offenders tell a variety of lies to themselves and others to justify their inappropriate and illegal behavior with a child.

As self-centered and manipulative as this behavior may be, these offenders generally have only a small number of victims, and once caught and convicted, they usually do not commit further sex offenses. However, it is very important to note that they <u>must</u> be processed through the legal system and be convicted, in order to ensure that the behavior stops. Families that cover it up and make it the "dirty little family secret" are only serving to perpetuate the offender's illegal sexual behavior, which sometimes spans generations of children.

Families who cover it up also clearly send the wrong message to the innocent child victim. Their secretive behavior tells the child that protecting the molester is more important than protecting the child who was victimized, which traumatizes the child victim even further. Part of what keeps the offender from doing it again is that everybody knows about it, they are being monitored through the court and probation department, and there are now serious penalties for being caught doing it again. Once these secrets are finally out in the open, parents and other adults are better able to prevent further sex abuse of this victim, as well as other potential victims within the family. Parents then refuse to allow grandpa to have unsupervised access to vulnerable children within the family, and they certainly do not leave small children alone with him anymore.

This knowledge and an atmosphere of openness about the offender's crimes are crucial for monitoring and protecting children within the family. The family has to admit that the molestation did indeed happen, grandpa is guilty, and the child isn't lying. It is also important to note that most incest offenders genuinely care for their victims. Once they are convicted, they can usually be helped to understand that what they did was harmful to the child, and they do want to stop, because they do not want to further victimize children they love.

Can You Recognize a Sexual Offender?

Most people think they could pick a sex offender out of a group. They must stand out as ugly, frightening, mean, weird, or usually effeminate in appearance. That is far from the truth. Child molesters succeed again and again, because they look like everybody else. How often do we hear someone say something like this? "He couldn't possibly do something like that. He's such a nice man. He's a churchgoing pillar of the community."

Except for their sexual desires and behaviors, child molesters are pretty much like everybody else. That's the scary part. Although some child molesters are shy and socially inadequate, others are quite successful and socially adept. We have all heard of the cases where priests, Boy Scout leaders, Little League coaches, youth leaders, or popular teachers have been child molesters, much to everyone's great surprise. In fact, many child molesters engage in jobs, do volunteer work, or have hobbies that bring them into contact with an ongoing pool of potential child victims, while appearing to be pillars of the community. That is what makes them so dangerous. They are just like everybody else. They are trusted members of our families and our communities.

While it may be reasonable for parents to warn their children about the stranger who tries to lure them away with gifts and candy or drag them off into their car, parents should not be lulled into a false sense of security once their children learn their lesson about how to handle themselves with strangers. This lesson is sometimes called "stranger danger," and it is an important lesson to learn, but it's only a small part of the much bigger problem of child molestation.

Not All Sex Offenders Are Alike

While there are many commonalities among sex offenders, not all sex offenders are alike. They come in all shapes, sizes, colors, and ages. They are juveniles and adults, males and females, kindly and sadistic, retarded and intelligent, handsome and unattractive. However, there are some differences in the types of offenses committed by people of different age or races.

Many child molesters engage in what we call "grooming" of their victims. They begin with something that is very innocent and completely nonsexual, such as talking with the victim or inviting him to jump on his backyard trampoline or swim in his pool. From there, he touches the child in a nonsexual manner, maybe rubbing his neck or back or having the child sit on his lap to read a story. Often they wrestle on the floor in a common roughhouse manner, sometimes "accidentally" slipping his hand in the child's crotch area or under the child's shorts. Those behaviors are usually ignored, because it appears unintentional. This touching or wrestling gets the child accustomed to being touched or grabbed, so the child will not be frightened when the offender later touches the child to satisfy his sexual impulses. The touching gradually becomes more intrusive but is so gradual that the child does not fear what is happening or think that it is bad or weird.

Often, the offender looks for excuses to be naked in the presence of the child or for the child to be naked in his presence. This can take the form of showering with the child, bathing the child, or swimming naked. Sometimes he offers to help the child in the bathroom or allows the child to "accidentally" observe him while he is not fully clothed. This gradually allows the child to become accustomed to nudity in the presence of the adult offender.

Another ploy is to invite the child to view pornographic videos, books, or magazines with him, which helps to desensitize the child to nudity in the presence of the adult offender. Typically the nudity in the magazines or videos that the offender shows the child are fairly conventional heterosexual pictures. This is part of the slow, grooming process in which the offender invests his time. If the offender immediately jumped in to showing a young boy some gay porn, the child would probably freak out. Instead, these offenders take their time to allow the child to become accustomed to nudity and sex itself, before moving onto more deviant pictures or overt sexual behavior.

Sometimes these offenders engage the child in games that have nudity as a consequence. A common game used for these purposes is "Truth or Dare." Although many healthy, well-adjusted people once played this game as a child or teenager, this game has a very different purpose when played by a child molester. The rules of the game are that one person asks a second player a question. The second player must either answer truthfully, or accept the dare and do whatever he is told to do. For child molesters, the dare involves removing some item of clothing or performing some sexual act, but it's all done in a casual, joking manner at first. One ingenious child molester devised a way of turning the harmless child's card game, "Old Maid," into a game of strip poker. When a player lost a round, he had to remove an item of clothing. The game later progressed to where the player who lost was required to perform a sex act on the other player.

The more dangerous child molesters are the ones who are patient and willing to take time with this grooming process, to ensure later success when they try to get the child to engage in more overtly sexual behavior with them. There's no reason for most adult offenders to force a child to participate in sexual behaviors, because child victims are always easy to find. If one child does not go along with these tactics, the offender just moves onto another child who is more receptive to these devious and manipulative sexual exploitations.

It is rare for child molesters to engage in physical violence against their child victims, and those who do are sadistic sex offenders. Sadistic child molesters are extremely dangerous. The explanation for this is actually quite simple. As I mentioned previously, it is so easy for child molesters to gain access to a child victim through manipulation, bribes, and promises, that if an offender physically harms or terrorizes a child to gain compliance, it is because he enjoys it. This type of offender gets sexually excited by the emotional and physical suffering and the fear that his victim experiences, rather than by the sexual contact itself. There are no known mental health or criminal justice interventions to deal with these sexual sadists, except to remove them from society for the protection of others. If they are returned to the community, they have a high likelihood of committing more violent offenses. Fortunately, this type of sex offender is rare. Regardless of the particular type of sex offender, hopefully, the more we know about these sexual predators, the better prepared we and our children will be to protect ourselves against them.

Not All Child Molesters Are Men

I refer to the offenders in this book as 'he', because males comprise the vast majority of sex offenders. However, approximately 5% to 10% of sex offenders are females, and this number is likely to be an underestimate, because of the double standards that seem to apply. The sexual molestation of a male by a female, especially if the offender is only a child or adolescent, is likely to go unreported. When female children and adolescents are lured into sexual activity by an older male offender, society is more likely to recognize the predatory nature of these offenses and the lack of social and sexual maturity of the female victim. However, when males are the victims of older female offenders, society often views that as "getting lucky," and it simply isn't taken as seriously as offenses where the victims are female.

In my practice, I have also noticed a trend for female offenders to be more psychologically disturbed than their male counterparts, although I have not seen this documented in the scientific literature. Because of their relatively small number, little research has been done regarding the characteristics of female sex offenders.

What we know so far is that females who commit sex offenses as juveniles almost always have histories of severe neglect and both sexual and physical abuse. Because of their backgrounds of severe neglect and abuse, these young girls have serious psychological problems, they tend to have a poor response to treatment, and they are more likely than their male counterparts to commit more sex offenses in the future. The sad fact is that the criminal justice system and the mental health system are ill-equipped for handling such severe problems with female sex offenders, and it is not clear whether to treat these girls as victims or perpetrators. They are usually treated as both, but without much success.

Not All Child Molesters Were Sexually Abused As Children

Although there is a popular fable that children who are sexually abused automatically become adult child molesters themselves, that is not true. Although children who are abused may mimic that behavior with other children, they rarely continue that behavior through their adult lives. However, many adult child molesters have learned to claim that they were sexually abused as children, hoping to get sympathy from the court, after they are caught.

Convicted adult sex offenders have no higher rate of being sexually abused as children than other convicted criminals. However, people who commit sexual abuse do tend to have a higher rate of emotional abuse and physical abuse in their childhood. That suggests that the effects of emotional and physical abuse of a child may have even more severe, long-term consequences than the effects of sexual abuse. Although most people understand the need for children to receive counseling when they have been sexually abused, they may not realize that it is equally important to provide counseling for children who have been physically and emotionally abused.

Internet Offenders

When I started using the Internet in the early 1990's, it was not as popular a means of communication as it is today. The software technology was difficult to learn and not very user-friendly. However, today's point-and-click Windows software is so easy to use that it has become an essential part of social interaction and communication for most U.S. teens. In fact, children and teens usually know much more about this technology than their parents, who haven't taken the time to acquaint themselves with it. Over the past decade, the Internet has become a very popular tool for talking with old friends and making new ones, and there are chat rooms and websites designed for meeting people with any imaginable interest.

Chat rooms are group meeting in cyberspace, where strangers and friends can share information. There are chat rooms that cater to every sexual fantasy you ever heard of and to some you could never imagine. Even in the chat rooms that are not specifically designated for sexual conversation, the conversation frequently becomes sexually provocative and sometimes sexually explicit.

When a person wants to communicate with only one specific individual in the chat room, he sends an "Instant Message," which is viewed only by the recipient of that message. If that person responds, they end up having a private conversation between the two of them. People can even exchange photos of themselves and others, which are sent as attachments to these messages. There are also webcams that send images in real time. These are cameras that show the person's image, while they are chatting over the Internet.

However, anyone who has ever gone into one of these chat rooms knows that people commonly lie about their personal information and the photos that they exchange. People often claim to be younger, older, and more attractive than they are. If your new Internet chat friend asks for your photo and you're not particularly photogenic, you can send a photo of your daughter instead, or your neighbor, or simply pass on an attractive photo that another stranger sent to you the day before. Unless you're sending real-time images via a webcam, no one will be the wiser, as long as these meetings are limited to cyberspace.

Every day, hundreds of thousands of people chat with people whom they have never seen in person. Some want to wile away a few lonely hours and others are simply curious. Some are desperately lonely people who are too shy to meet in person, or insecure people who don't have the social skills or the confidence to say things in person that they are willing to say to a stranger in a chat room or with an Instant Message. Some feel unattractive or uninteresting, so they pretend to be someone they are not. For many people, the Internet is a form of fantasy entertainment, because they have no intention of ever meeting any of these cyber-friends in person. It's a way for lonely people to connect, even if the connection is only a cyberspace fantasy relationship.

But for some desperate people, it is a way to meet someone with the hope that a face-to-face romance will follow. I know of couples who met over the Internet and later married or lived together. Although I can't say much for the quality or longevity of any of the ones I know, I have heard that it has worked for some couples. I also know of marriages that ended, when one spouse discovered that the other was engaging in a cyberspace romance with a stranger. In either case, it has become an extremely popular means for both adults and teens to meet potential romantic partners. In this chapter, I refer to teens as using this technology to make friends and meet new people. However, it is clear that the age of the Internet user is becoming increasingly younger, and even elementary school children have been lured by child molesters.

The Internet allows a person to communicate with multiple potential partners at the same time without having to get dressed up to go to bars, churches, community activities, and other meeting places. That makes the selection process quicker and easier. However, because the Internet permits complete anonymity, no one ever really knows who is at the other end of a conversation, unless they meet in person.

Child molesters have also become very adept with this technology. Through the use of the Internet chat rooms, Instant Messages, and certain websites such as **www.myspace.com,** sexual predators no longer have to work as hard to insinuate themselves into the lives of children and teens. These websites are used by children and adolescents to meet their peers, and they often post very personal information and photos that can be accessed by anyone who cares to view it. By viewing the information that children post on these websites, Internet predators can quickly view hundreds of profiles each night and screen for just the right characteristics that they prefer. They no longer have to walk to playgrounds, ball fields, schools, or swimming pools to find new victims. The Internet saves them the time, requires less footwork, and preserves their anonymity during the grooming process. A child molester can take a walk in cyberspace, without leaving his home or office. [And, yes, a lot of this is done from the office computer.] The offender can screen through dozens, even hundreds of conversations in one sitting and quickly determine the age and gender of their next potential victim and receive a photo.

They carefully screen potential victims and choose the ones who seem most vulnerable and unsupervised. Young girls or boys who are living with a grandparent or a single working parent are often good targets. Typically, Internet offenders begin by engaging in casual, nonsexual conversation. They show interest in the teen's friends, school, music, and shopping sprees. They sympathize with the child who complains about his parents or problems at school. Neglected and emotionally needy children respond readily to this outpour of time and attention, and the Internet predator knows how to make these children feel special. The more skilled offender uses these conversations to gain the victim's trust, while assessing the likelihood that their potential victim is really who he or she claims to be and not another adult impersonating a child or a police officer trying to entrap him.

Internet predators are highly skilled at mimicking adolescents' ever-changing Internet language, with all of their school-age slang, Internet lingo, and special Internet abbreviations. They even learn to misspell words, just like the kids do, to appear more appealing to the child or teenage victim. Some sex offenders lie about their age at first, but after they gain the trust of their potential victim, they admit that they are a much older adult and ask the child if it is still okay for them to continue chatting together. By then, the teen has begun to like the predator and look forward to the attention and profuse compliments that the sex offender typically offers, so the teen is willing to make the necessary adjustment to the new information about their Internet friend's age.

Usually the Internet predator broaches the subject of sex by asking whether the child has a boyfriend or girlfriend, then asking what kinds of things he or she has done with their boyfriend or girlfriend. That allows the offender to ask about the child's sexual experiences and attitudes and to get the child comfortable with talking about sex, without revealing his intentions. Gradually, the conversations become more sexually explicit, and the offender starts to make sexual suggestions about the two of them together, perhaps done in a joking manner at first. Depending upon the juvenile's responses, the sexual aspect of the conversation then becomes more serious. Some Internet sex offenders accomplish all of this in the first conversation, sometimes even within minutes, while others communicate for several weeks before asking for a real life meeting to have sex.

As part of my evaluation of Internet predators, I review the entire transcript of their Internet chat or Instant Message conversations. Then I count the number of minutes that it took the offender to initiate sexually explicit conversation with intended victim, as well as the number of minutes it took him to ask the victim to meet to have sex. Unlike most sexual predators who meet their victims in person then slowly groom them until they are receptive to their sexual advances, skilled Internet predators are so good at spotting vulnerable children that they can close the deal within minutes after initiating the first chat conversation. However, most of these offenders chat with their victims at least three to five times over the course of a few days or weeks, before they arrange to meet to have sex. It is less common for an Internet sex offender to take the time to groom the victim over the course of several months, before arranging to meet for sex.

Given the speed with which some of these Internet predators take action, my advice to parents is to talk to their children about the dangers of meeting strangers over the Internet and make sure that both children and parents know who is at the other end of their child's Internet conversations. While many adult sex offenders are willing to reveal their true age to their victims, parents and teens should not automatically assume that the person who claims to be an adolescent boy is not a 47-year-old sexual predator. If a stranger of any age asks about their sexual behaviors or tries to arrange a meeting, children should tell their parents and never meet in person with a stranger whom they met on the Internet. Children and adolescents should never exchange a picture or provide personal information to a stranger over the Internet. Often children do this inadvertently by telling the offender where they go to school, the names of their friends, or when they meet friends for sports or other activities. Armed with all of those pieces of seemingly harmless information, a sex offender can figure out when and where to show up in person to lure the child away or take the child by force.

Unlike most child molesters who may spend weeks or even months grooming their victims,

Internet predators often move much more quickly. By using the Internet as a tool, they can quickly interview and screen for children who are more readily receptive to their sexual interests without having to bother with a lengthy grooming process. The Internet allows predators to quickly "interview" potential victims, discard those who are not immediately receptive, and move on quickly to the next potential victim.

A Real Danger: Fixated Pedophiles

Ralph's Life Story [According to Ralph]

While incest offenders have the lowest recidivism rates among all types of sex offenders, the two types of sex offenders with the highest recidivism rates are sadistic rapists and fixated pedophiles with a sexual preference for young boys. Some aspects of the following story are so bizarre that, if it were a fictional story, no one would believe that a person could be so depraved. However, this is a story about a very real person, and all of the details of this story are true. Only his name has been changed.

*Ralph was a handsome, muscularly built, 36-year-old White man with sandy brown hair and a pleasant smile. Ralph and his housemate *Joe were both involved in a singles group at a church, and they were using the church group as a means of luring young boys. It was through that church group that they met 12-year-old *Neal. Ralph took Neal to a family cabin in Kentucky, and Neal often stopped at the two men's home after church. Ralph started by giving the boy massages, then progressed to showing him pornography. Pornography is often used by sex offenders to acquaint children with sexual images, while reducing their discomfort with sexual behavior. It's part of the grooming process and is a highly calculated and manipulative tactic.

Ralph also made up many fantastic stories about himself to impress the boy. He said he had been a football star and that he was in the Navy. He told some adults that Neal was his son, which kept them from becoming suspicious about Ralph's affection toward the boy. Ralph and his partner Joe sometimes told parents that they were both in the Secret Service, and many parents believed them. It made the parents feel good to know their children were in such trustworthy hands.

Through their pattern of lies and deception, these two men managed to hide their sexual exploits even from other members of the church group, who were unaware that Ralph was a pedophile. Many sex offenders feel very safe about joining church groups, then using them as a cover for selecting victims from the congregation. Child molesters expect religious people to be easier to deceive, because church members want to believe in the goodness of others. They are less inclined to suspect sinister motives in adult males who want to spend enormous amounts of time with young boys. Even when a child molester is caught in the act, they are more forgiving and more inclined to fall for the child molester's manipulative excuses about a bad childhood and pleas for forgiveness. Many people believe them, because they want to believe that people can change for the better, but I'm skeptical about sudden religious conversions after they are caught. These offenses were not reported to police at that time, which left Ralph free to continue molesting other boys.

A couple years later, Ralph was arrested for showing pornography to an 11-year-old boy and a 12-year-old boy. The boys also said that Ralph had "a whole shelf of guns going down the wall" and he "used nun chucks and acted like a Ninja," all of which were very effective lures for attracting young boys. Many of the other neighborhood children went to Ralph's house to jump on the trampoline in Ralph's back yard. He spent a great deal of money and effort to design and equip his home in the best possible manner to lure young boys and to keep them coming back for more. To decrease their suspicions about his intentions and to put the boys at ease, Ralph told them that he had a son who was in the fifth grade, which was close to the boys' own ages.

Following his arrest, he said that he was sorry and would never do it again. The detective on the case requested a psychological evaluation and said, "Something is not quite right." However, because Ralph was cooperative with authorities and expressed remorse, and because this was his first conviction, he was put on probation with no jail time, and he had to go to counseling.

Counseling obviously did not help. A few years later, he was arrested for his molestation of another 12-year-old boy, *Jimmy. In an attempt to deceive others about his relationship with Jimmy, Ralph had told numerous people that his wife and son were killed in a car accident. However, Ralph had never been married and never had a son. At times, Ralph even introduced his victims to others as his son, to keep others from becoming suspicious about how much time he was spending with these young boys.

Jimmy's life was far from ideal. He lived for awhile with his grandmother who beat him and sometimes made him eat dog food. Then he lived with his mother and he was beaten by his stepfather. His father was in prison for raping

Jimmy's sister, and his stepfather was accused of sexual misconduct with that same sister. It is not a coincidence that many sex offense victims have had a tragic or neglectful home life. These are the children who are most vulnerable to the influence and control of the adult pedophile, and the more chaotic the home life, the less likely the adults will discover what the pedophile has been doing with their child. Ralph was convicted of two counts of Rape, and he was sentenced to nine years on each count and the sentences were run consecutively for a total of 18 years in prison.

What Parents Need to Know About Child Sexual Abuse

It is nearly impossible to talk about child molesters and sex offenses without occasionally using language that some people will find objectionable. This book uses words that cause some people to feel uncomfortable, but I believe that speaking openly and directly is necessary to gain an understanding of the way that sex offenders behave and think and how to protect children from sexual abuse. If the use of certain words or the open discussion of sexual issues makes some people feel uncomfortable, they probably put down this book long ago.

That is unfortunate, because that is exactly what child molesters want them to do. Child molesters depend upon your discomfort and confusion about sexual abuse. They want you to look the other way, rather than talk openly and directly about sexual issues. They want you to see them doing things that are sexually inappropriate, then convince yourself that what you think you saw was really something more benign, because you can't face what might actually be happening. And most of all, child molesters depend upon your silence and they depend upon you doing nothing, so they can continue to sexually abuse children.

If parents can't even talk to other adults about sex, if they get upset by reading the words on a page, how can they expect to talk to their children about protecting themselves from child sexual abuse? Don't fool yourselves. Kids know when their parents are uncomfortable talking about things. If they sense that you're not able to hear it, they won't feel comfortable coming to you with their questions or for help when someone tries to do something sexually inappro-priate to them.

A much better approach would be to start talking with children about sex at a very young age, in much the same way that we talk to children about brushing their teeth and taking a bath. Children need to know the proper names for body parts, in case they someday need to communicate information to their parents or even police about the part of their body where a person tried to touch them. Parents should keep open the lines of communication about sex, rather than making it a taboo subject that children should not know about.

This can be very difficult for some parents. But if they want their children to be able to tell them about something sexual that is happening to them, and if they want their children to be able to tell them when they are being sexually abused, then children need to feel comfortable talking about sex to their parents. And parents need to learn how to feel comfortable talking about sex to their children.

What could be more heartbreaking for a parent than learning that when their daughter was eight years old, her babysitter was molesting her, but she told no one until several years later, because she couldn't talk to her parents about sex? What about the young boy, who waited until he was an adult to confide that his stepfather sexually abused him as a child?

If a child believes that his parents will not understand or will get upset by talking about sexual matters, that conversation will not take place. Surveys completed by adults, who were asked about their sexual experiences as children, indicate that as many as 80% of sexual assaults against children were not reported. The fact that frank discussions about sex may be uncomfortable for parents should not prevent them from educating and protecting their children from sexual abuse.

There are many resources available at your local library for assisting parents with these conversations. These vary from books that are more user-friendly to those that are more scientific and research-oriented. Many websites offer free or low cost books and pamphlets that are designed to assist parents in talking to their children about these issues.

What children should also be taught is that these are their private body parts and that no one else should be touching them without good reason, such as a bath or medical exam. In fact, I believe that children should be taught that no one should touch any part of their bodies without the child's permission, including their shoulders, hands, back, arms, feet, or legs. Parents should teach their children to respect their bodies and their choices about who can touch them. A child should believe that his body is his own, and no one touches him unless he wants to be touched. It is far too commonplace for adults to insist that a child give old Uncle Joe a big hug or allow grandpa to give them a slobbering kiss, even when the child clearly is uncomfortable and does not want to do it.

Without realizing it, these parents are grooming their children to become ideal victims for a child molester. They are teaching their children to ignore the fact that they don't want to be physically intimate with an adult, and that making the adult happy is more important than the child's discomfort about the unwanted touching. Child molesters love compliant children who have been taught to do whatever adults tell them to do without regard for their own feelings and anxieties. Children who never say "No" to adults make great victims.

Instead, parents should teach their children to have respect for their own bodies, not just their private parts, and to respect their feelings. If a child doesn't want to give the kindly old man a kiss or a hug, then the child should not be forced to do it just "to be nice." Sex offenders really like "nice" kids who do everything that adults tell them to do.

To keep their communities safe, adults need to learn what to do about people who are sexually abusing children and have not been caught. Children should not have to try to stop sexual abuse all by themselves. They can't. Adults need to learn to trust their instincts when someone is behaving strangely around children and to learn what action to take when they think that a child has been or is being sexually abused.

With all the misinformation permeating today's society, some relevant questions should be posed as follows:

[1] What is sexual abuse?

[2] Who abuses children?

[3] What are some of the signs to look for when

other adults are with our children?

[4] What are some ways to prevent sexual abuse of children?

[5] What is healthy sexuality in children and adolescents?

[6] What are some of the signs that a child has been sexually abused?

[7] What to do when you think a child has been sexually abused?

What is Sexual Abuse?

If you aren't exactly sure what sexual abuse is, you're not alone. About half the people in this country don't know what it is. Child sexual abuse is sexual activity with a child by an adult, an adolescent, or a much older child. All sexual activity between an adult and a child is sexual abuse, and it's illegal in all 50 states. Although it is clear that sex between an adult and a child is illegal, when it comes to sex between an adult and an adolescent, legal definitions vary from one state to another. Sometimes the definition of a sex offense requires a minimum number of years difference between the age of the offender and the age of the victim. For example, it might seem unreasonable to prosecute an 18-year-old man for rape for having consensual sex with his 17-year-old girlfriend. In Ohio, if there are more than four years difference between the age of the offender and the victim, the offense is a felony, but if there are fewer than four years difference, it's a misdemeanor. However, when the sexual activity is between adolescents or between children, the distinction between experimentation and a crime is not as clear.

Child sexual abuse includes both touching and non-touching behaviors. Some of these touching behaviors include:

1. Touching a child's sexual areas [penis, vagina, anus, buttocks, testicles, breasts] for sexual grati-fication or for any other unnecessary reasons.

2. Forcing a child to touch the adult's sexual areas or playing sex games with the child.

3. Putting things into the child's mouth, anus, or vagina, including penis, tongue, fingers, or objects.

Touching a child to bathe or clothe him is obviously not sexual abuse. However, many child molesters use nonsexual behaviors as a cover for sexual activities. This includes the father, step-father, or babysitter who finds far too many excuses to rub the child's genitals with salve, or uses the bath as an opportunity to insert his fingers into the toddler's vagina. I even know of fathers who continued to bathe children as old as ten years old, simply because that excuse met the abuser's needs for a cover story for his continued sexual abuse.

Child molesters who force, coerce, or manipulate a child into touching sexual areas of an adult's body routinely claim that they were teaching the child about sex through demonstration. Some profess that it is better for the child to learn about sex from someone who loves her, rather than from some boy who just wants her for her body. That excuse usually comes from a close family member. Most sexual abusers, especially child molesters, go to amazing lengths to deny, minimize, and justify their grossly inappropriate and illegal sexual behaviors with children.

The most common object that is put into a child's vagina or anus is the offender's fingers, although all kinds of objects have been used. Often, the abuser claims that he was simply trying to give the child pleasure, while claiming that he derived no sexual pleasure from it himself, because he was certainly not attracted to a child. I evaluated one male babysitter who made up a special strip poker game that required the loser of each hand of cards to remove an article of clothing then allow the winner to touch him there. Turning physical touching and sexual contact into a game is a common tactic for child molesters. It allows the child to become accustomed to sexual touching without arousing the child's fears or suspicions that there is something wrong the behavior. As I said before, sex offenders are often willing to spend an enormous amount of time preparing the child for sexual activities, moving from nonsexual talk and relationship-building to increasingly more sexually intrusive activities.

Some non-touching sexual behaviors include:

1. Showing pornography to a child. Those people who followed the Michael Jackson trial will recall that he had a collection of sexually explicit magazines and books in his bedroom and that they were accessible to the young boys who slept in his bed with him. When adults show a child pictures of adults engaged in sexual acts, it desensitizes the child to the activities in the pictures and makes it easier for the child molester to move to his next step in the grooming process.

2. Exposing one's genitals to a child. This can come about in many different ways, but usually the initial exposure is made to appear appropriate or accidental. One way of enticing young boys into the home is to collect items that are especially exciting

boys that age. Some abusers have model car collections, some have pets, others have a swimming pool or trampoline in the backyard and they allow neighborhood children to swim and play, while the child molester "supervises."

For example, one child molester whom I evaluated made a habit of remaining naked in his own home. Then he would invite neighborhood boys into the house to perform well-paid chores or to look at his sword collection. He would insist that young boys strip when they entered his home, after the boys finished mowing the lawn or performing other outdoor jobs that might have gotten them wet or dirty. He then required them to shower, and he would offer to help dry the boys with a towel, although all of the boys were old enough to dry themselves.

Other child molesters act as though they have just gotten out of the shower. When they "accidentally" expose themselves to a young boy, they explain that nudity is natural and that no one should ever be ashamed of their body. While this is a perfectly acceptable attitude, it is more questionable when the unmarried male next door is prancing around naked in front of your ten-year-old son or daughter!

Some offenses that fall into this category are

subtle, while others are much more blatant. For example, one stepfather had the habit of unzipping his pants and exposing his penis to his 12-year-old stepdaughter. Then he would hold her head close to his penis without actually touching it and force her to look at his penis, until he released her head. And, of course, there is the well-worn excuse that the adult is simply providing sex education to the child by showing them what adult genitalia look like.

3. Taking pictures of a child in sexually explicit positions. Today, Internet access and digital cameras make this a particularly widespread problem, because it is relatively easy to take a picture and then trade it with other like-minded people by e-mail or through Internet chat rooms that advertise their sexual preferences. It is also easy to buy miniaturized spy cameras over the Internet, then strategically place these cameras in the bathroom or bedroom. The pictures are fed into a television screen, from which they can be saved to a video-tape.

I have evaluated many men who were eventually caught taking movies or photos of family members while they bathed, undressed, or used the toilet. Once apprehended, it is often the case that large collections of sexually explicit pictures and other sexual paraphernalia are found in their homes. One man claimed that he was taking photos of his 14-year-old stepdaughter because she was anorexic, and he had to spy on her to make sure she was not making herself vomit into the toilet. That story lost credibility, when it was discovered that his file cabinet was filled with photos of his step-daughter, along with a soiled pair of her panties and a used tampon. Clearly, what is disgusting to one person can be sexually arousing to another.

4. Watching a child undress or use the bathroom. This goes along with the previous item. Just watching for purposes of one's own sexual gratification, even if photos are not taken, is child sexual abuse.

5. Viewing or downloading nude photos of children from the Internet, other than for educational or legal purpose. Just viewing these materials, even if someone else took them, is against the law. Many people incorrectly believe that it is okay to view child pornography in their own homes on the Internet. Even if they realize it is wrong, they tend to believe that no one will ever find out. Many child molesters have been arrested after they or their wives took the computer to a repair shop, not realizing that the images could be discovered by the repairman and would be reported to police. Some have been caught when they sold

their computers, without realizing that they had not deleted all of their files. Yet others have been arrested for something unrelated to the sexual material on their computers, but when their computer was seized in the process, child pornography was discovered on the computer, resulting in additional charges.

6. Having a child watch sexual acts, either in person or on video. While many abusers use pornographic movies to entice young boys to their homes or to get children more accustomed to sexual behavior, I have encountered men who actually performed sex acts with an adult female in the presence of one or more children. In some cases, these served two purposes. Although the man was not particularly sexually aroused by the adult female, the presence of the children made the act sexually arousing. And again, it is part of the grooming process, making children more desensitized to sexual behavior by watching it.

Who Abuses Children?

Most people think of a child sexual abuser as the stranger who jumps out from behind a bush and grabs a child or the stranger who offers them candy to take a ride with them. However, in 90% of the cases of child sexual abuse, the abuser is someone that the child knows and trusts. Most child sexual abusers are family members — fathers, stepfathers, grandfathers, uncles, or close friends and acquaintances such as neighbors, Boy Scout leaders, elementary school teachers, babysitters, bus drivers, coaches, ministers, Big Brothers, or anyone else who has a lot of contact with children. They're usually not mentally ill, and they don't look different from anyone else. The only difference between them and other adults is that they have a sexual interest in children.

Most people who commit sexual offenses against children also have a sexual interest in adults, but a small portion of these offenders prefer only children and they have no sexual interest at all in adults. Although these offenders comprise a small minority of child molesters, they tend to have many child victims over their lifetimes. Because they are not a family member, friend, or acquaintance, they may have less regard for the safety of their child victims.

It is also important to note that while strangers who abduct children for sexual purposes are extremely rare, these are the most dangerous type of child molester. These offenders are likely to harm or even kill a child. These are the offenders whom most parents have in mind when they warn their children about the danger of going off with strangers. Many school and police departments have "stranger danger" programs to teach parents, teachers and children how to avoid this threat. However, it should be kept in mind that these types of sex offenders are rare. The ones who are most likely to present a danger to children are people that the child already knows and trusts.

When Other Adults
Are With Your Children

As you know by now, child molesters don't look any different from anyone else. So what are some of the signs that a person might have a sexual interest in children?

1. He spends most of his time with children and he has little or no interest in spending time with adults. [Beware of the Peter Pan syndrome!]

2. He often takes several different children or one special child on overnight outings or trips.

3. He frequently babysits several different children without charging money, just because he likes being with children or because he wants to do their parents a favor. Please don't overreact. This is not the close family friend who offers once to help, when the parent is in dire need. This is the guy in the neighborhood who always seems to be babysitting for parents and tends to spend more time with children than with adults.

4. He always seems to manage to get time alone with children or with one special child. He works

hard to find time when no one is likely to interrupt.

5. He hangs onto a child, kisses, hugs, tickles, wrestles with the child, even when the child seems to dislike it or seems uncomfortable with it.

6. He buys a child an expensive gift or several smaller gifts for no reason.

7. He shows too much interest in a particular child's sexual maturity, commenting frequently on the child's sexual development or asking questions about the child's sexual behavior. He may actively interfere with the child's normal sexual development. This is a common theme that I see with adolescent girls, who have been sexually abused by their fathers or stepfathers. These girls later complain that he did not allow them to engage in normal social and dating activities, most likely because he was jealous of boys her age and wanted her to himself. When sexual comments are made in the presence of the child and make the child feel uncomfortable, there may be a legitimate cause for concern. This is especially true if the person making the comments is a neighbor or someone who is not a family member.

8. He frequently walks in on a child when he or she is going to the bathroom, showering, or dressing. Although mistakes can happen, especially

in a large family that shares small spaces or just one bathroom, habitual mistakes may not always be accidental.

9. He shows an inappropriate sexual interest in children, either by viewing or talking about child pornography, preferring to have his adult sexual partner dress up as a child to "turn him on" during sex with the adult partner, or talking about his sexual fantasies that involve children. He may also make fun of a child's body parts or call a child sexual names that are completely inappropriate for a young child, such as calling a young boy a "stud" or a young girl a "whore."

Caution: Don't just assume that everyone who expresses a friendly interest in children is a child molester. Some people are involved with children, just because they care in a completely nonsexual, appropriate way. Don't be paranoid, but trust your gut. Child molesters depend upon your fear of making false accusations and your uncertainty, so they can continue having access to children. If you see behavior between an adult and a child that makes you feel uncomfortable or that seems to make the child feel uncomfortable, trust your instincts and DO NOT allow that adult to have unsupervised access to your child. If that adult has access to other children, consider telling other adults about your concerns. And if you believe that a child has been molested, report that person to authorities. Child molesters depend upon your silence and upon you doing nothing, so they can continue molesting children.

Why is child molestation so prevalent?

Child molestation is so prevalent because most child molesters are not reported to anyone. There are several reasons why most sex crimes against children are not reported:

Children tell no one, because there are no adults the child trusts enough to talk about sexual matters. No adult in his life has ever shown signs of being comfortable with hearing about sexual matters. If parents want their child to tell them about the person who is behaving in an inappropriate sexual manner with him or her, they have to make the child feel comfortable talking to them about sexual matters.

Child molesters are very adept at choosing their victims. They tend to choose compliant children who need special attention. They convince the child that they have a "special secret relationship" and that the relationship would end, if they told anyone else about it.

They may give the child gifts and take them on

special outings, when the child's parents cannot afford it or don't make the time. They bribe children to remain secret about what is happening to them.

If bribes don't work, the offender may threaten the child. They say that if the police learn about it, their mother will be seen as a "bad mother" and that the child will be placed in foster care, because he has "bad parents."

If the child threatens to tell, the offender usually stops and moves to his next victim, but he also may threaten to harm the child, his parents, or his entire family.

One way or another, child molesters are very skilled at finding children who are willing to keep their secrets. Sometimes, even when the child tells, it goes no further than a parent. No authorities are ever contacted. That's because most child molesters are a family member or a close friend, someone the child and the child's family know and trust. Families prefer to handle this problem among themselves, so that the adult does not get into trouble with the law.

Sometimes family members decide to give the child molester a second chance, or they think they are doing the right thing by not making a big deal out of it, mistakenly believing that it will harm the child more to testify in court against the family member than to pretend that it didn't happen. They believe that if they ignore the problem, it will go away. Even worse, often when a child reports the abuse, the parents don't believe the child. The child may even be punished for "lying" the family member or beloved community leader. The child realizes that the situation is hopeless and that no one will rescue him, and the abuse continues.

A Word About "Stranger Danger"

Strangers who try to lure children away for sexual purposes comprise a very small portion of child molesters, but most parents have had the talk with their children about the dangers of leaving their home, school, or play area with strangers. Unfortunately, this lesson provides parents with a false sense of security, for two reasons. One, most child molesters are not strangers. They are people the child knows and trusts. Two, although young children came recite what they are supposed to do, if a stranger tries to convince them to get into their car, few children actually follow that advice in real life situations.

When I was about ten or eleven years old, my mother left me at home alone for one or two hours. She carefully warned me to lock the door after she left and to open it for no one. I knew I should not allow anyone into the house, when she was not there. I lived in the country and we had no neighbors, but a highway cut through the hills a couple hundred yards from our house. A man knocked on the door, and I ignored him at first. Then he knocked harder and said he had car trouble and needed to use the telephone to call for help. I could see his car pulled off to the side of the road, so I thought that was sufficient evidence that he was telling the truth. I allowed the man into the house, and he made his call. As he was leaving, he said, "You shouldn't let strangers in the house, when your mother isn't home." I already knew that. My mother would never have believed that I would have opened that door to a stranger, but she was wrong. The man needed my help, and I couldn't refuse him.

That's how predators lure children from their homes. These predators are skilled at knowing how children think. A man limps or uses a cane and asks a child to help walk him to his car. Or he says he has puppies in his van and asks the child if she wants to pick one out for herself. Or he drops his packages next to his car, and the child leaves his yard to help the stranger pick them up.

Children do not learn these lessons simply by being told what to do. They need to role-play these scenarios with their parents, then talk to their parents about what they thought and felt, when the stranger made them an offer they couldn't refuse. By acting out some of the possible ploys that might be used to lure them away, parents can help the child with what to say and how to act. Most children do not realize that adults seldom ask a child for help. Adults ask someone who is older and stronger, not a small child, but that is not usually obvious to a child. It is very difficult for a child to yell and run away, which is what they are usually instructed to do, when someone is asking them for help. So parents should not be lulled into a false sense of security, just because they have had this talk with their children. Repetition and role-playing are key to putting this knowledge into action.

How Parents Can Prevent Child Sexual Abuse

Teach toddlers the proper names for their sexual body parts, at the same time that they are learning the words for their other body parts. Teach them the proper words - penis, vagina, buttocks, anus, testicles, etc. If parents are uncomfortable at first, they should practice saying these words aloud to themselves, practice in front of a mirror, then practice on another adult. Parents must become comfortable with it or the child will sense their discomfort.

Talk to your children about sex, starting from a very early age. There are books to help, if you are not comfortable, and I strongly suggest reading them, because they can help you find a more comfortable way to handle the topic. Answer your children's questions openly and honestly, but don't overload them with information. Keep your answer simple and direct. If you are not comfortable, practice talking about these things with an adult. Children need to know that there is nothing wrong with talking about these things with you, so they will not feel comfortable coming to you with questions or coming to you when an adult has done something that makes them feel uncomfortable.

Teach your children about appropriate and inappropriate touches, and teach them that it is okay to say "No" to adults and anyone else who tries to touch them in ways that make them feel uncomfortable. Depending upon the child, this should happen between the ages of three and five. For example, when a stepfather or grandfather hugs a child, and the child squirms and wants to get away, don't tell the child to go along with it, because the adult loves him. That teaches a child to ignore his own feelings about physical intimacy and to be compliant with adults, regardless of his own feelings. Remember, child abusers prefer compliant children. Let your child know that it is okay to say "No" and make him feel supported in his own decision. This also sends the message to other adults that the parents are watching out for their child.

Teach your children that they should not agree to keep secrets about adults touching them, and tell them that this is not a sign of a "special relationship." This is a special tool of child molesters. They encourage children to believe that they have a "special relationship" that no one else should know about, and they persuade children to keep secrets from their friends, teachers, and family. Because some children are not getting enough parental time and attention at home, they enjoy feeling special and go along with these secrets. By age five, a child should be ready for a discussion about "good touches" and "bad touches."

Listen when your child tries to talk to you about something that seems difficult to talk about. Children find it difficult to talk about these things too.

Look for warning signs of inappropriate behavior between adults and children and act to protect the child. Don't be paranoid, but don't be blind either. Adults who ask children to keep secrets from their parents, give children expensive gifts or money, frequently have the child spend the night, and have no apparent adult relationships deserve further scrutiny.

Watch for other warning signs:

a. Your child receives telephone calls from men you do not know or makes calls to numbers you do not recognize.

b. She receives packages or gifts from people you do not know.

c. He quickly turns the computer off when you show up or changes to the screensaver.

d. You find pornography on your computer.

e. He uses an online account that belongs to someone else.

f. She spends many hours on the computer at night, when you are asleep.

Adults should become aware of physical and behavioral signs that a child may have been sexually abused. Some of these include developing a sudden fear of men, becoming overly secretive or reclusive, or having expensive gifts or money that the child cannot explain. If a child has unexplained bruises, bleeding, or redness of the genitals, mouth, or anus, or if the child experiences pain or genital sores, a physician should be consulted, and it might be recommended that the child be tested for sexually transmitted diseases.

Be careful, however. There are many mental health professionals who claim that almost any kind of emotional distress or behavioral change that a child could ever experience is associated with sexual abuse. Some of these symptoms are too far-reaching and could be attributed to many other sources of distress or turmoil in a child's life, such as seeing parents argue, moving to a new school, having a fight with a friend, or the death of a pet.

Know the adults who are spending time with

your children, especially babysitters and mom's new boyfriend. Mothers, do not be so desperate for a man in your life that you allow someone you hardly know to move in with you and your children. The same goes for allowing the young man who just got evicted from the upstairs apartment to stay with you, until he finds a place to live. I'm not saying to be uncharitable toward others. But make sure you know people well, before you allow them unsupervised access to your children.

Discuss safe Internet use with your child. Parents should spend time with their child online and monitor their child's Internet use. If parents are not familiar with the Internet, learn. There are books and other resources available to help.

Keep the computer in a place where it can be easily monitored and position the screen so it is visible to others. Keeping the computer in the parents' bedroom ensures that the child cannot use the computer without permission, even while the parents are asleep, although it may not be easily monitored during the day.

Use parental controls and blocking software, but don't rely solely upon them. Stay personally involved. Maintain access to the child's online account and let your child know that you will check it randomly.

If you suspect that the person with whom your child has been chatting on the Internet is trying to seduce or lure your child, notify local law enforcement. Soliciting minors for sexual activities is a crime.

Advise children to be suspicious of adults who seek help from children. Adults rarely ask children for help, and a child should not feel obligated to obey, just because it's an adult. Children who have been taught to be polite and to ignore their own feelings are more likely to become victims of unscrupulous adults.

Check to see whether your local school or police department provides a "stranger danger" program to teach children and parents more about how to avoid this less common but more dangerous type of child molester.

Call the local Sheriff's Office to learn about child sex abusers in your community. However, the list of offenders that law enforcement agencies can provide will include only a small portion of sex offenders who are living in your community. At least one in three sex offenses against children are never reported to anyone, and not all convicted sex offenders are covered by the sex offender reporting requirements [Megan's Law].

The last thing that I want to do by writing this

book is to promote paranoia about the sexual abuse of children. There's enough of that in this country already. If in doubt, talk to other parents, teachers, or other adults about your concerns.

Advice for Teens

Never give out your name, address, e-mail, phone number, or any other personal information to a stranger.

As tempting as it may be, never tell a stranger where you go to school. Casually mentioning that you have soccer practice after school on Thursday or that you are wearing a red sweater to school on Friday can provide predators with sufficient information to find you.

Do not list personal information as part of your personal Internet "profile."

Never send or receive pictures from strangers. Do not post your photo online.

Never respond to a sexually suggestive message.

Never arrange to meet an Internet "friend" any-where, not even in a public place.

What To Do When You Suspect Sexual Abuse

All instances of sexual abuse MUST be reported to authorities, either to the local police department, Sheriff's Office, or Children Services Bureau. The law requires that it be reported and failure to report the sexual abuse of a child is a misdemeanor offense. However, the more important reason to report it, is that it will not stop unless it is reported. Child molesters depend on people being confused about what they see, giving the molester the benefit of the doubt, remaining silent, and feeling too embarrassed to do anything about it, so they can continue molesting children.

Most child molesters do not repeat their offenses, following their conviction and completion of mandatory legal sanctions; e.g., incarceration, community control following release from prison, but they must first be identified and prosecuted. No more than 10% of incest abusers repeat their offense after they are convicted, but many continue to abuse children within the family for many years until they are convicted. Once convicted, they are usually incarcerated or sent to treatment programs, and they are monitored through the Courts for compliance with the rules of probation or parole.

There is a small subgroup of pedophiles who are not treatable. They must be stopped, convicted, monitored, and identified within the community to protect our children. Regardless of whether it is the incest offender or the fixated pedophile, sex offenders cannot be stopped until they are reported to authorities, either law enforcement or to the local Child Protection agency. Parents are doing no one a favor by deciding to "keep the problem within the family" or by giving the local priest or Boy Scout leader a break or by simply encouraging the offender to get counseling or treatment. Many offenders stop only because they have been convicted, and child sex offenders need to be monitored. Their past and future victims need to be protected from them, and only the Courts can do that effectively.

Parents and teachers should not automatically dismiss a child's reports of sexual abuse, simply because the alleged abuser is a respected member of the family or of the community or because the child is perceived as a troublemaker. If you suspect that a child is being sexually abused, report it to law enforcement or to the county Children Services agency. If you have questions about what you have seen, report it. The worst that can happen if you are wrong is that an innocent person is investigated and the allegation is determined to be unfounded. When you report a possible incident of child sexual abuse to a county Child Protection agency, your name will not be revealed. The worst that happens if you fail to report it and you are wrong is that a child, and possibly many other children, will continue to be sexually abused.

Although the sexual exploitation of children and adolescents is a growing concern, there is no need to be frightened or to overreact. Parents, teens, and children can begin to combat this problem through knowledge and open exchange of information. Reading this book may be the first step for many parents and teens. My advice to parents is to read and learn. Go to the local library, take an Internet class, search the Internet for helpful information, and talk to other parents. But most of all, talk openly and honestly with your children about this problem and about how they can protect themselves against sexual predators within the community and on the Internet.

About the Author

Dr. Bobbie Hopes is a forensic psychologist who earned her doctorate degree from Miami University of Ohio. She has worked in jails, prisons, and courtrooms for 25 years, and has evaluated thousands of criminal defendants ranging from bad check writers to sexual predators and serial killers.

Over the past ten yers, she has completed comprehensive psychological evaluations of nearly two thousand juvenile and adult sex offenders. As an expert on sex offenders, she routinely conducts workshops for judges, probation officers, prosecutors, and attorneys.